PSALM 119

THE ROAD LESS TRAVELED

A 22-Day Devotional to Explore the Significance, Relevance, Richness, and Authority of God's Word.

Rev. Dr. Bryan K Crawl

Copyright © 2024 by Rev. Dr. Bryan K Crawl

Self-Published by Rev. Dr. Bryan K Crawl

All rights reserved. This book or any portion thereof may not be reproduced or used in any manner whatsoever without the express written permission of the publisher except for the use of brief quotations in a book review.

Printed in the United States of America

First Printing, 2024

ISBN 979-8-9918048-1-3 (pbk.) ISBN 979-8-9918048-0-6 (eBook)

Library of Congress Cataloging-in-Publication Data is on file at the Library of Congress, Washington, DC.

Website: www.drbryanbooks.com

Contact: conversationsdrb@gmail.com

TABLE OF CONTENTS

1. DEDICATION vii
2. FOREWORDS 1
3. INTRODUCTION 5
4. WHY THE ROAD LESS TRAVELED 9
5. FACTS ABOUT PSALM 119 11
6. THE CHALLENGE 15
7. MY PRAYER 19
8. THE 22-DAY CHALLENGE PART ONE 21
   - DAY #1: ALEPH 21
   - DAY #2: BETH 23
   - DAY #3: GIMEL 25
   - DAY #4: DALETH 27
   - DAY #5: HE 29
   - DAY #6: WAW 31
   - DAY #7: ZAYIN 33
   - DAY #8: HETH 35
   - DAY #9: TETH 37
   - DAY #10: YODH 39
   - DAY #11: KAPH 41

9. REFLECTION QUESTIONS 43

10. AUTHOR'S INSIGHTS 45

11. MY PRAYER 49

12. THE 22-DAY CHALLENGE PART TWO 51
- DAY #12: LAMEDH 51
- DAY #13: MEM 53
- DAY #14: NUN 55
- DAY #15: SAMEKH 57
- DAY #16: AYIN 59
- DAY #17: PE 61
- DAY 18: TSADHE 63
- DAY #19: QOPH 65
- DAY #20: RESH 67
- DAY #21: SHIN 69
- DAY #22: TAW 71

13. AUTHOR'S INSIGHT 73

14. FINAL THOUGHTS 79

15. MY PRAYER 81

16. ABOUT THE AUTHOR 83

17. REFERENCES 85

DEDICATION

This precious, biblically inspired offering is dedicated to my grandparents, Robert (Bobby) and Hazel Mae Doster. They not only introduced me to Christ, but they also lived out their faith right before me. Until I see you again!

PSALM 119

THE ROAD LESS TRAVELED

"A 22-Day Devotional Challenge to Explore the Significance, Relevance, Richness, and Authority of God's Word."

FOREWORDS

"I read The Road Less Traveled 22-Day Challenge with great interest. Bryan is a colleague, pastor of a sister church, and a dear friend of mine. I have loved his faithful service to Christ and his church and have been encouraged in so many ways by his life and passion.

The Road Less Traveled is, of course, based on Psalm 119. Psalm 119, the longest chapter in the Bible, can be hard to get through! Each verse contains a gem about the Word of God, leading to the possible question, "How many ways can you tell us about the importance of God's word?"

Bryan has answered that question. The Road Less Traveled represents a thoughtful, and thought-provoking, dialogue that both remains faithful to Scripture and also provides a contemporary reading. His style reads like a conversation, as if two people were sitting down and discussing the Psalm together.

I commend this challenge to all, to read, enjoy, think, meditate, and grow!"

Senior Pastor, Author Jeff Arnold First Presbyterian Church, Beaver, PA.

"In religion, as in war and everything else, comfort is the one thing you cannot get by looking for it. If you look for truth, you may find comfort in the end; if you look for comfort, you will not get either comfort or truth, only soft soap, and wishful thinking to begin with and, in the end, despair." - C.S. Lewis

That quote by C.S. Lewis provides a fitting backdrop as I reflect on how Reverend Dr. Bryan Crawl and I crossed paths as active-duty veterans, navigating the final stretch toward that coveted "golden ticket"—a retirement check on the first of every month. As middle-aged men, we found ourselves chasing a dream many boys carry from childhood: becoming firefighters. We were men with a lot of baggage, carrying the weight of anger and past debauchery. Though once lost, we had been found by a wonderful Savior and were now seeking the truth.

If I shared the story of how our paths crossed, it would become clear that God's sovereignty should never be questioned. The words of Jude 24 about our Lord keeping us from stumbling resonate, because, as only the Potter can, He shaped our journeys to run parallel, teaching us the true meaning of laying down our lives for our friends and proving that "A cord of three strands is not quickly broken."

Along the way, I had the privilege of watching and cheering on a man with the intellect, attitude, and passion to go from having no degree to earning a doctorate in 9 years. A natural leader, he balanced countless responsibilities—managing the chaos of real life, responding to fire calls in the war theater, and tirelessly serving young people in need back home. This included chaperoning all-nighters with funky-smelling middle schoolers, unclogging toilets, and driving a bus full of elementary students to after-school programs. And after all that, he would still make time to hustle over and teach the Lord's Prayer to kids in the projects.

There was never a meal we shared when the words, "This is the day that the Lord has made; let us rejoice and be glad therein," did not pass his lips, even in the face of personal challenges that would have crippled many a good man. The road less traveled might better be called a rugged goat path, leading only to places where eagles dare to soar. "Mr. B," as I affectionately call him, has been walking that path, doing the right thing for so long that at Tiger Pause, no one will ever ask, "How come there ain't no brothers on the wall?" If you're unsure what that reference means, this might just be the devotional you need to read."

"On the Jericho Road" is a song written in 1928 by Don and Marguerete McCrossan and recorded by Elvis Presley. "On the Jericho Road, there's room for just two, No more and no less, just Jesus and you,
Each burden He'll bear, each sorrow He'll share. There's never a care for Jesus is there."

Rev. Crawl's devotional will help you come to that understanding.

Matthew (Mr. Matt) Nance
CEO Tiger Pause Youth Ministry Beaver Falls, PA.

I met Pastor Crawl in 2017 when he sought the pastorate of Second Baptist Church, Rochester, PA. I was the chair of the pastoral search committee which eventually presented Pastor Crawl to the congregation for consideration. Pastor Crawl and first lady, Apryl, have exhibited a love for the congregation and community that shows in the time and energy they give to whatever their hands touch. Pastor Crawl is committed to preaching, teaching, and serving the flock of God. His service to the community is evident in his work with youth through Tiger Pause Youth Ministry and as coach of the Beaver Falls High School golf team.

As a Deacon of Second Baptist Church, I have had the privilege of serving with Pastor Crawl and this book is just an extension of his commitment to the work of God's kingdom. This book challenges the reader to meditate deeply on God's Word. I encourage the reader to take the twenty-two-day challenge and experience something new in your relationship with God.

Anthony C. Comer, Ph.D
Chair, Department of Engineering Professor of Chemical Engineering Geneva College, Beaver Falls, PA

INTRODUCTION

WHY IS THE ROAD LESS TRAVELED

Let me start with a confession. Almost twenty-five years into my Christian journey and eleven years into vocational ministry, it was not until recently that I traversed and meditated on the profound verses of Psalms 119 with any completeness of thought or seriousness of study. I think many believers, who, if honest, would also share in my confession that we are either too impatient or we perceive ourselves as too busy to spend any valuable time spiritually navigating the 176 verses of this Psalm. In all honesty, I would often overlook or ignore these vibrant passages for another less tedious offering, such as Psalm 23 or some other well-known and shorter contribution from the psalmists.

In the past, when it came to this Psalm, I would cherry pick certain verses such as 119:105 *"Your word is a lamp to guide my feet and a light for my path,"* or 119: 103, *"How sweet your words taste to me; they are sweeter than honey."* And while cherry-picking is not a sin, the spiritual crime is that I have never done a serious and complete reading of this often-bypassed Psalm. One sister in my congregation labeled Psalm 119 as the forgotten Psalm, and, as I measure the reaction of a recent sermon on Psalm 119, I would have to concur with her assessment. Speaking of that sermon, it was during a time of study on just a few verses that I finally read this Psalm in its entirety with a serious approach of meditation and reflection—this time also produced a season of repentance in my heart. I say repentance due to my impatience and excuse of busyness that had me initially overlook a Psalm that emphasizes the Bible's Significance, Relevance, Richness, and Authority in the lives of those who say we desire to follow God's Word in totality. I believe the study and meditation of this Psalm should also bring others to repentance. My hope is that anyone who would accept the challenge of this biblically inspired offering births a sincere yearning to apply the theme of this Psalm. If taken seriously, this mindset to apply the Word of God in our lives in its completeness would produce a longing desire to transform our minds to address, on some scale, many of the unbiblical traditions and practices that exist in the body of Christ, especially here in America.

At this point, anyone with any knowledge and understanding of Psalm 119 might be inclined to conclude that my last statement is a bit off the mark or quite a stretch. With 176 verses wholly devoted to God's Word, one might ask, "What do 176 verses about the Significance, Relevance, Richness, and Authority of God's Word have to do with anything we see in our politically charged, socially confused, and morally corrupt culture?" If you didn't get it, this was an attempt at a rhetorical question. And if you didn't at least smile at my feeble attempt at humor, I would tell you that the 176 verses of Psalm 119 have everything to do with the current divisive climate we see in our culture, which has unfortunately infiltrated the body of Christ.

Right now, many in the body of Christ have bought into and sold out to political, social, and moral ideologies on the right and left that are inconsistent with the Word of God. This bought-in and sold-out ideology of various worldly constructs says that if we disagree with one another, we are now enemies. The divide in the church is primarily attributed to the current cultural attitude, which is, again, totally inconsistent with God's Word.

Many who have taken one side or the other have filtered their moral and social views through sources of misinformation or rhetoric of one extreme or another, both of which are usually totally devoid of and inconsistent with the proper application of the Word of God.

In his book *"Strength to Love,"* Rev. Dr. Martin Luther King coined a label for those Christians who genuinely adhere to God's Word. He called them *"Transformed non- conformists."* In one illustration, MLK says, *"...most people, and Christians in particular, are thermometers that record or register the temperature of majority opinion, not thermostats that transform and regulate the temperature of society."* (King, 1977) In the divisiveness we see in the body of Christ in the 21st century, I hope many will agree that we need more *"Transformed non-conformists."* Transformed non-conformists are those who will be so brave in a time of political, moral, and social conformity to follow the *precepts, testimony, commandments, judgments, ways, laws, and statutes* of God's Word. Transformed non-conformists are those true believers who will bypass the status quo, which, at times, presents the normalization of inconsistent behaviors that do not follow the standards contained in God's Word. I believe that adopting a transformed non- conformist attitude and mindset prompts a believer to filter the political, moral, and social issues that confront the culture and the church through the prism (Reflector of light) of the Word of God. Only then may we understand that our focus should be on the moral condition of our culture rather than political outcomes to direct and teach biblical righteousness.

I will use the example of abortion and say that too many in the body of Christ view this issue through the lens of a secular worldview instead of through the Word of God. When this is done, the problem becomes political instead of moral. When the issue of abortion is first filtered through the prism of God's Word, it becomes moral before it is political and, therefore, more significant in scale because it encompasses teaching (Matthew 28:19) moral and sexual purity along with other biblical standards.

When God's Word is pushed to the forefront of the Christian mind, the shackles of a secular worldview fall off and are replaced with a Christian mindset. I believe Psalm 119 directs or redirects the Christian to the Significance, Relevance, Richness, and Authority of God's Word and its role in the life of the believer and follower of Jesus Christ.

<u>WHY THE ROAD LESS TRAVELED</u>

My discovery of the significance of Psalm 119 was also around the time I learned of my family's first roots in rural Western Pennsylvania. As the story was told to me, my family was freed from slavery at a Virginia plantation. After receiving their freedom, they traveled and settled in the farm country of Western Pa. in a place called "Indian Run" located in Mercer County. The unsubstantiated story states that some of my family, those who could pass for white, stayed in Mercer Co. while the other darker-skinned members decided to move to New Castle, Pa. One of those who chose to leave Indian Run was my great-great- grandmother, Mary Allen. I would imagine that the migration to New Castle presented more opportunities due to the steel mills and a greater population of black folks.

Well, as it turned out, that was only part of the story. Our family discovered there was much more to our rich history. The motivation of the slave owner to free his slaves and purchase property for them in Pennsylvania is unknown. What is known is that the community where my family settled was founded by two white men who broke from the Presbyterian Church because of the church's reluctance to take a stand against slavery.

These two men founded a church called "White Chapel" that still exists today. They also created a small community where black and white families co-existed, some of whom were my ancestors.

This story resonated with me because here we see a few Christians who ignored the political and social norms of that time, which legalized and normalized the subjugation of human beings in a system called slavery. Brave people like these are why we had the abolitionist movement, the Underground Railroad, and this small community of formerly enslaved black people. These courageous souls put God's *precepts, testimony, commandments, judgments, ways, laws, statutes and Word* before man's laws, political ideologies, and the moral and social status quo of their time. What a debt of gratitude I owe to those two brave souls who put God's Word first and foremost in their lives. I owe them the deepest appreciation not just for helping to settle my first freed ancestors on American soil but also for providing a spiritual example of putting God and His Word first and persevering to apply those truths to their lives, no matter the cost.

When I consider the impact that these two courageous people had on my family's history, I stop and consider: What if a million Christians anywhere would place God's truth at the forefront of their worldview? What impact could that make on the body of Christ and the world today?

FACTS ABOUT PSALM 119

Psalm 119 has an anonymous writer; however, some scholars attribute it to Ezra. It is the longest of the Psalms and the longest chapter in the Bible. All verses, except for 1, 2, 3, and 115, are addressed to God. The genre of the Psalm is primarily wisdom literature, and its content includes elements of lament, praise, thanksgiving, and confidence.

It has been said that this Psalm's primary theme is the practical use of the Word of God in the life of the believer, which I believe harkens back to its being mainly wisdom literature. The aim of practical application may be examined in verses 9, 11, 92, 98, 105, 130, 133, and 176. Psalm 119:5, *"Oh, that my actions would consistently reflect your decrees!"* (NLT).

C.S. Lewis said of this Psalm, *"The Poem is not, and does not pretend to be, a sudden outpouring of the heart like, say Psalm 18. It is a pattern, a thing done like embroidery, stitch by stitch, through long quiet hours, for love of the subject and for the delight in leisurely, disciplined craftsmanship."* (Lewis, 1958)

Psalm 119 is also an acrostic. The word acrostic means a series of lines or verses in which the first, last, or other letters, when taken in order, spell out a word, phrase, or in this case, the Hebrew alphabet. In the case of this Psalm, the acrostic nature plays out as it takes the 176 verses and presents them in eight-verse increments, with each first verse of the new thought starting with the preceding letter of the Hebrew alphabet. The first verse, therefore, starts with the letter "A" and is entitled "Aleph." The second is "B" with the title "Beth."

Psalm 119 uses 8 different synonyms for God's Word, such as way(s) 13 times, law(s) 25 times, testimony 23 times, precepts 21 times, statutes 21 times, commandments 22 times, judgments 23 times, and Word 39 times. To sum it all up, that equals 187 times the Word of God is mentioned in this Psalm. With so many references to God's Word, the Psalmist is trying to tell us something about the importance of the Word of God in the lives of those who believe.

"Way" or "ways" (Hebrew- Derek)
"Law" or "laws" (Hebrew- Torah)
"Testimony" (Hebrew- 'edot)
"Precepts" (Hebrew- piqqudim)
"Statutes" (Hebrew- hiqqim)
"Commandments" or "commandment (Hebrew- miswot)
"Judgement" or "ordinance" (Hebrew- mosh-other)
"Word" (Hebrew- Dabar)

For the Bible exegete, the study of Psalm 119 leads to only one conclusion. That conclusion is that the Psalmist took 176 verses to place enormous importance on the Word of God. Now, some exegetes may be inclined to conclude that such emphasis leads to idolatry or that the attention given may be a bit redundant. However, with such prominence given to the Lord, this fact should dispel any inference to worship of the Word instead of its Author Almighty God.

As we approach Psalm 119, let the reader desire to *"Study to shew thyself approved unto God"* and *"Rightly divide the Word of truth"* (2 Tim. 2:15). As we, the readers, meditate on the facts of Psalm 119, I believe one would conclude that the Psalmist is saying we must do so using an academic and spiritual approach with a practical aim. We may examine this aim in the first two verses of this wisdom literature. Psalm 119:1-2, *"Blessed are the undefiled in the way, who walk in the law of the Lord! Blessed are those who keep His testimonies, who seek Him with the whole heart!"* (NKJV).

With practical application as our aim, Tony Evans said of Psalm 119, *"The entire Psalm is an appreciation for, celebration of, and dependency on the Word of God to enable us to properly negotiate the twists and turns of life."* (Evans, 2020)

THE CHALLENGE

The aim of this biblically inspired offering is to broaden the appreciation of the richness and importance of the Word of God in every believer who is bold enough to take this challenge. This challenge encompasses an examination of how the application of God's precepts plays out in our lives. This challenge may open the eyes of some to how culture can creep in and influence our thinking more than we may be aware of. Some believers may be challenged to change their opinions and approaches to the issues that confront our world today. If the application of God's Word is paramount, then each believer is challenged to take the issues that confront the church and the culture and filter them through the authority of Scripture.

The Greek word for authority is *exousia*, which means that we as believers give God's Word the final say in all matters. This authority therefore trumps human opinions and the status quo. When we challenge ourselves to place the Bible as our ultimate source, we can stand on its truth as if the Word of God is a lighthouse in the storms of moral chaos and confusion. When Scripture guides us, its light will lead us safely to the shores of righteousness. One of my personal favorites from Psalm 119 is verse 105, which reads, *"Your word is a lamp to my feet, and a light to my path"* (NKJV). Since John 1:1 declares that Jesus is the Word, we are to let Jesus and the

Word of God lead our lives devoid of conformity to the darkness of the world (Romans 12:2).

2 Timothy 3:16-17 states, *"All Scripture is given by inspiration of God, and is profitable for doctrine* (What is right), *for reproof* (What is not right), *for correction* (How to get right), *for instruction* (How to stay right) *in righteousness, that the man of God may be complete, thoroughly equipped for every good work"* (NKJV). Therefore, this challenge for more than a few will be to take a serious look at the fact that some, if not much, of our thinking and worldviews have been influenced by the world instead of driven by the Word. Romans 12:2 teaches us as believers this vitally important biblical principle: *"And do not be conformed to this world, but be transformed by the renewing of your mind, that you may prove what is that good and acceptable and perfect will of God" (NKJV).*

Recently, I spoke with a pastor who told me that about two hundred members left his church because they felt that their rights were being violated during the COVID pandemic due to mandatory mask requirements. This pastor told me that he was called names and met with much hostility over the issue of trying to keep his congregation safe. Whether an individual agrees or disagrees with this policy is not the issue; however, I ask what the response would be if applying the Word of God was paramount? Now I ask this general question, "Was the decision to leave influenced by a worldly construct or secular worldview, or was it influenced by God's Word?" If these members felt offended, where is the application of Colossians 3:13, which reads, *"Make allowance for each other's faults, and forgive anyone who offends you. Remember, the Lord forgave you, so you must forgive others?" (NLT)*. If these members felt their rights were being violated, where is the application of Galatians 5:13, *"For you have been called to live in freedom, my brothers, and sisters. But don't use your freedom to satisfy your sinful nature. Instead, use your freedom to serve one another in love?" (NLT)*. Or how about 1 Corinthians 10:31- 33, *"So whether you eat or drink, or whatever you do, do it all for the glory of God. Don't give offense to Jews or Gentiles or the church of God. I, too, try to please everyone in everything I do. I don't just do what is best for me; I do what is best for others so that many may be saved?" (NLT)*.

My point and my challenge are that we take the issues that confront us as believers of Jesus and filter them through God's Word so that our responses are biblically transformed instead of world conformed. If we desire to please God in all we do, if we desire to be able to stand before our King Jesus and say, *"I have fought the good fight, I have finished the race, I have kept the faith" (NLT)*, then we all as believers of Jesus are challenged to live by the *precepts, testimony, commandments, judgments, ways, laws, and statutes,* of God's Word.

My hope is that you take this challenge and develop a desire to be obedient to the Holy standards contained in God's Word. Through this challenge, we should all examine our thinking and application of God's Word in our lives, and where our thoughts and behaviors are offline, we must realign them to be in obedience to the authority of Scripture. I believe at this critical juncture in redemption history that we as individuals and as the body of Christ are challenged by the words of Dr. Martin Luther King. To be thermostats that regulate the moral temperature of culture rather than thermometers that record worldly ideologies driven by the prince of the air, Satan.

As you begin this challenge, I hope and pray that you will gain a greater appreciation of the significance Scripture plays in the lives of Jesus's followers. I pray that each day, you take away something that will inspire you to make God's Word the supreme standard by which all human conduct, creeds, and opinions must be tried.

<u>MY PRAYER</u>

Lord, please bless those who would endeavor to take this challenge. Please open all hearts and minds to obey the guidance Your Word provides. Lord, I ask You to plant seeds of knowledge that will grow and produce a mighty harvest of holy behaviors and righteous actions.

Lord, challenge us all to place Your Word as our final and ultimate authority. Place in us all a desire to know, study, and apply Your Word as we endeavor to be the light that shines in the darkness of this world. Lord, bless our obedience to Your Word that the world may see our good works and glorify You, oh, Lord, in heaven.

Lord, I pray this prayer in the mighty and matchless name of Jesus Christ. Amen!

THE 22-DAY CHALLENGE
PART ONE

DAY #1: ALEPH

1. Joyful are people of integrity, who follow the instructions of the Lord.

2. Joyful are those who obey his laws and search for him with all their hearts.

3. They do not compromise with evil, and they walk only in his paths.

4. You have charged us to keep your commandments carefully.

5. Oh, that my actions would consistently reflect your decrees!

6. Then I will not be ashamed when I compare my life with your commands.

7. As I learn your righteous regulations, I will thank you by living as I should!

8. I will obey your decrees. Please don't give up on me!
SYNONYMS USED FOR God's Word: Instructions v.1, laws v.2, commandments v.4, decrees v. 5, 8, commands v. 6, regulations v. 7.

QUESTIONS

1. What verse(s) stood out the most in this section?

2. Write that verse(s) down, read it several times today, and meditate on its significance.

3. Consider how you would apply this section to your daily living. What part of these verses do you think will be the most challenging for you and why?

4. What do you think the psalmist meant in verse 5? How does this verse change or consistently shape your actions?

Note: *You are encouraged to journal your notes, thoughts, meditations, and insights. This will allow you to track your progress and examine how your approach, opinions, and application of God's Word may change over these next 22 days.*

For the E-reader please use a notepad or some other means to journal your way through the challenge.

JOURNAL

Notes- Thoughts- Meditations- Insights

PSALM 119
THE ROAD LESS TRAVELED

DAY #2: BETH

9. How can a young person stay pure? By obeying your word.

10. I have tried hard to find you—don't let me wander from your commands.

11. I have hidden your word in my heart that I might not sin against you.

12. I praise you, O Lord; teach me your decrees.

13. I have recited aloud all the regulations you have given us.

14. I have rejoiced in your laws as much as in riches.

15. I will study your commandments and reflect on your ways.

16. I will delight in your decrees and not forget your word.

SYNONYMS USED FOR God's Word: Word v. 9, 11, commands v. 10, decrees v. 12, 16, regulations v. 13, laws v. 14, commandments v. 15.

QUESTIONS

1. **What verse(s) stood out the most in this section?**

2. **Write that verse(s) down, read it several times today, and meditate on its significance.**

3. Consider applying this section to your daily living. What part of these verses do you think will be the most challenging for you and why? Read the section again and then read Joshua 1:7-8.

4. What would introducing today's youth (v. 1) to the Word of God take? What have you done to engage today's youth with God's Word? Consider giving or sending a Bible to a young person.

JOURNAL

Notes- Thoughts- Meditations- Insights

PSALM 119
THE ROAD LESS TRAVELED

DAY #3: GIMEL

17. Be good to your servant, that I may live and obey your word.

18. Open my eyes to see the wonderful truths in your instructions.

19. I am only a foreigner in the land. Don't hide your commands from me!

20. I am always overwhelmed with a desire for your regulations.

21. You rebuke the arrogant; those who wander from your commands are cursed.

22. Don't let them scorn and insult me, for I have obeyed your laws.

23. Even princes sit and speak against me, but I will meditate on your decrees.

24. Your laws please me; they give me wise advice.

SYNONYMS USED FOR God's Word: Word v. 17, instructions v. 18, commands v. 19, 21, regulations v. 20, laws v. 22, 24, decrees v. 23.

QUESTIONS

1. What verse(s) stood out the most in this section?

2. Write that verse(s) down, read it several times today, and meditate on its significance. Read Philippians 4:8-9.

3. Consider applying this section and verse(s) to your daily living. What part of this section or the verse(s) you chose do you think will be the most challenging for you and why?

4. How can we as believers be overwhelmed (v. 20) with a desire to follow the Lord's Word? Consider this statement, as we see many Christians today who know God's "Way" but don't follow it.

JOURNAL

Notes- Thoughts- Meditations- Insights

PSALM 119
THE ROAD LESS TRAVELED

DAY #4: DALETH

25. I lie in the dust; revive me by your word.

26. I told you my plans, and you answered. Now teach me your decrees.

27. Help me understand the meaning of your commandments, and I will meditate on your wonderful deeds.

28. I weep with sorrow; encourage me by your word.

29. Keep me from lying to myself; give me the privilege of knowing your instructions.

30. I have chosen to be faithful; I have determined to live by your regulations.

31. I cling to your laws. Lord, don't let me be put to shame!

32. I will pursue your commands, for you expand my understanding.

Synonyms Used for God's Word: Word v. 25, 28, decrees v. 26, commandments v. 27, instructions v. 29, regulations v. 30, laws v. 31, commands v. 32.

QUESTIONS

1. What verse(s) stood out the most in this section?

2. Write that verse(s) down, read it several times today, and meditate on its significance. Memorize the verse(s) that stood out the most to you. Read Psalm 1:2.

3. Consider applying this section and the verse(s) you chose to your daily living. What part of this verse(s) do you think will be the most challenging for you and why?

4. How do you think we, as believers, lie to ourselves? Is it to justify sin (v. 29)? How does the Lord confront us with His Word on these occasions, and more importantly, do we/you listen? Read 1 Corinthians 10:13.

JOURNAL

Notes- Thoughts- Meditations- Insights

PSALM 119
THE ROAD LESS TRAVELED

DAY #5: HE

33. Teach me your decrees, O Lord; I will keep them to the end.

34. Give me understanding and I will obey your instructions; I will put them into practice with all my heart.

35. Make me walk along the path of your commands, for that is where my happiness is found.

36. Give me an eagerness for your laws rather than a love for money!

37. Turn my eyes from worthless things, and give me life through your word.

38. Reassure me of your promise, made to those who fear you.

39. Help me abandon my shameful ways; for your regulations are good.

40. I long to obey your commandments! Renew my life with your goodness.

Synonyms Used for God's Word: decrees v. 33, instructions v. 34, commands v. 35, laws v. 36, word v. 37, regulations v. 39, commandments v. 40.

QUESTIONS

1. What verse(s) stood out the most in this section?

2. Write that verse(s) down, read it several times today, and meditate on its significance. Read Psalm 1:2-3.

3. Consider applying this section and verse(s) to your daily living. What part of this verse(s) do you think will be the most challenging for you and why?

4. How do you think verses 33 and 39 correlate? If we follow what it says in verse 33, will we have a problem with verse 39? Are you working through the Word to confront anything *shameful* in your life?

JOURNAL

Notes- Thoughts- Meditations- Insights

PSALM 119
THE ROAD LESS TRAVELED

DAY #6: WAW

41. Lord, give me your unfailing love, the salvation that you promised me.

42. Then I can answer those who taunt me, for I trust in your word.

43. Do not snatch your word of truth from me, for your regulations are my only hope.

44. I will keep on obeying your instructions forever and ever.

45. I will walk in freedom, for I have devoted myself to your commandments.

46. I will speak to kings about your laws, and I will not be ashamed.

47. How I delight in your commands! How I love them!

48. Honor and love your commands. I meditate on your decrees.

Synonyms Used for God's Word: word v. 42, regulations v. 43, instructions v. 44, commandments v. 45, laws v. 46, commands v. 47, 48.

QUESTIONS

1. What verse(s) in this section is the most challenging for you?

2. Write that verse(s) down, read it several times today, and meditate on ways to follow its precepts daily.

3. Reflect on how the first 6 days have challenged and stretched your thinking about applying God's Word in your daily living. Write down your thoughts.

4. In verse 45, the psalmist speaks of walking in freedom. What does this verse mean to you? Read John 8:31-32 and reflect on how devoting (v. 45b) ourselves to the Word brings freedom.

JOURNAL

Notes- Thoughts- Meditations- Insights

PSALM 119
THE ROAD LESS TRAVELED

DAY #7: ZAYIN

49. Remember your promise to me; it is my only hope.

50. Your promise revives me; it comforts me in all my troubles.

51. The proud hold me in utter contempt, but I do not turn away from your instructions.

52. I meditate on your age-old regulations; O Lord, they comfort me.

53. I become furious with the wicked, because they reject your instructions.

54. Your decrees have been the theme of my songs wherever I have lived.

55. I reflect at night on who you are, O Lord; therefore, I obey your instructions.

56. This is how I spend my life: obeying your commandments.

Find and write down the synonyms used for God's Word:

QUESTIONS

1. **In verses 49 & 50, the psalmist mentions a promise; what do you think the promise is? Read Deuteronomy 31:8, Joshua 1:7-9, Hebrews 13:5.**

2. What verse(s) caught your attention in this section and why? What part of this verse(s) do you think will be the most challenging for you and why?

3. In verse 53, the psalmist states that he is furious with those who do not follow the instructions of the Lord. Do you share this frustration? How do you settle this issue? Read Colossians 3:13, Matt. 28:19.

4. In verse 56, the writer says he will spend his life obeying the Lord's commandments. If you share this commitment, what is your formalized plan to follow and know all the Lord's commands?

JOURNAL

Notes- Thoughts- Meditations- Insights

PSALM 119
THE ROAD LESS TRAVELED

DAY #8: HETH

57. Lord, you are mine! I promise to obey your words!

58. With all my heart I want your blessings. Be merciful as you promised.

59. I pondered the direction of my life, and I turned to follow your laws.

60. I will hurry, without delay, to obey your commands.

61. Evil people try to drag me into sin, but I am firmly anchored to your instructions.

62. I rise at midnight to thank you for your just regulations.

63. I am a friend to anyone who fears you—anyone who obeys your commandments.

64. O Lord, your unfailing love fills the earth; teach me your decrees.

Find and write down the synonyms used for God's Word:

QUESTIONS

1. **In verse 59, the psalmist says that he pondered the direction of his life. Is the direction of your life in accordance with God's laws? Have you turned *from* any wrong direction and turned *to* follow God's laws? Read 2 Chronicles 7:14.**

2. What verse(s) caught your attention in this section and why? What part of this verse(s) do you think will be the most challenging for you and why?

3. Write that verse(s) down, meditate on it during the day, and ponder why it stood out to you.

4. In verse 64, the writer asks the Lord to teach His decrees; how might the Lord teach us? Read 1 Corinthians 2:10-12, 2 Timothy 3:16-17.

JOURNAL

Notes- Thoughts- Meditations- Insights

PSALM 119
THE ROAD LESS TRAVELED

DAY #9: TETH

65. You have done many good things for me, Lord, just as you promised.

66. I believe in your commands; now teach me good judgment and knowledge.

67. I used to wander off until you disciplined me; but now I closely follow your word.

68. You are good and do only good; teach me your decrees.

69. Arrogant people smear me with lies, but in truth I obey your commandments with all my heart.

70. Their hearts are dull and stupid, but I delight in your instructions.

71. My suffering was good for me, for it taught me to pay attention to your decrees.

72. Your instructions are more valuable to me than millions in gold and silver.

Find and write down the synonyms used for God's Word:

QUESTIONS

1. **In verse 67, the psalmist mentions the Lord's discipline. Can you think of a time when the Lord disciplined you and why? How did obedience to God's Word get you back on track?**

2. Do you think there are any similarities between verses 67 and 71? Consider how suffering can be good for us. Read Psalm 51.

3. Consider and meditate on verse 69. What is your course of action when encountering arrogant people who lie against you? Are your actions in line with God's Word? Read Leviticus 19:18, Matthew 5:11-12, Luke 6:27-28, Romans 12:20- 21.

4. Today, meditate on verse 65; think back on how you had to be disciplined (v.67) by the Lord. Now consider how it was good and how the Lord has grown and stretched your faith. Now give Him thanks!

JOURNAL

Notes- Thoughts- Meditations- Insights

PSALM 119
THE ROAD LESS TRAVELED

DAY #10: YODH

73. You made me; you created me. Now give me the sense to follow your commands.

74. May all who fear you find in me a cause for joy, for I have put my hope in your word.

75. I know, O Lord, that your regulations are fair; you disciplined me because I needed it.

76. Now let your unfailing love comfort me, just as you promised me, your servant.

77. Surround me with your tender mercies so I may live, for your instructions are my delight.

78. Bring disgrace upon the arrogant people who lied about me; meanwhile, I will concentrate on your commandments.

79. Let me be united with all who fear you, with those who know your laws.

80. May I be blameless in keeping your decrees; then I will never be ashamed.

Find and write down the synonyms used for God's Word:

QUESTIONS

1. **In verse 78, the psalmist asks the Lord to bring disgrace to arrogant people who have lied about him. Think about how you have dealt biblically**

with people who lied on you. Did you pray for both the Lord's justice and for the person or people? Read Matthew 5:44.

2. Once again, the psalmist mentions the Lord's discipline. Think of a time when the Lord's discipline helped you and why. Now, thank Him again!

3. In verse 79, the psalmist asks the Lord to let him be united with godly people who know and follow His laws. Take a moment to think about those closest to you. Now, ask yourself if they know and follow the Lord's ways. What might you do to help those who know the Lord but do not follow His ways?

4. Take a moment of meditation on this portion of Psalm 119 (discipline and obedience). Review the psalmist's words of obedience to the Lord's *commands, laws, regulations, Word, instructions, and decrees.*

JOURNAL

Notes- Thoughts- Meditations- Insights

PSALM 119
THE ROAD LESS TRAVELED

DAY #11: KAPH

81. I am worn out waiting for your rescue, but I have put my hope in your word.

82. My eyes are straining to see your promises come true. When will you comfort me?

83. I am shriveled like a wineskin in the smoke, but I have not forgotten to obey your decrees.

84. How long must I wait? When will you punish those who persecute me?

85. These arrogant people who hate your instructions have dug deep pits to trap me.

86. All your commands are trustworthy. Protect me from those who hunt me down without cause.

87. They almost finished me off, but I refused to abandon your commandments.

88. In your unfailing love, spare my life; then I can continue to obey your laws.

Find and write down the synonyms used for God's Word:

QUESTIONS

1. **In verse 81, the psalmist says that he is worn out from waiting for a response from God. Have you ever been in a comparable situation? Think about what Scriptures gave you hope or what passages**

REV. DR. BRYAN K CRAWL

could help you to be better equipped to deal with those situations if they were to arise again in your life. Read Psalm 27:14, Isaiah 40:31.

2. In this section of Psalm 119, there are several verses of lament. Can you think of a time of lament in your life? Now consider if it matured your faith and how God's Word brought reassurance.

3. In verse 87, the psalmist says that he refused to abandon the Lord's commandments. Can you think of a time that you held to God's Word despite an unfair situation? What would you do differently today?

4. Take a moment of meditation on this portion of Psalm 119. Review the psalmist's words of lament and his commitment to follow the Word of the Lord. How has your commitment to God's Word grown through this time of study, meditation, and reflection?

NOTE: *At this point, the terms used to identify God's Word should be familiar to you. At this stage in the challenge, consider how you now view all the words attributed to God's Word. Do you have a greater appreciation of God's **precepts, testimony, commandments, judgments, ways, laws, statutes, and Word?** Today, meditate on how the challenge has strengthened your application of God's Word in your life, and consider how you will approach the next 11 days.*

REFLECTION QUESTIONS

1. At this halfway point in the challenge, take a moment and consider how your view of God's Word has changed.

2. Will your new appreciation of the Word change how you study or commit to daily devotions?

3. Has the psalmist affected how you now view God's *ways, laws, testimonies, precepts, statutes, commandments, judgments, and Word?*

4. Take a moment of meditation on the first 11 days of this challenge. Pick out your favorite verses and go over them throughout the day. Consider how you will approach the remainder of the challenge.

JOURNAL

Notes- Thoughts- Meditations- Insights

AUTHOR'S INSIGHTS

I sincerely hope and pray that at this point in the devotional you have been challenged to focus or refocus on how the Scriptures are to be our guiding light as believers of Jesus Christ. If we agree that God's Word brings illumination to life, then we should pray that the Lord, through the Holy Spirit, would continue engaging our minds. With the engaging of our minds, we let the truth of Scripture travel those nine long inches downward to permeate our hearts. There, the Word intermingles with the spirit within us to apply those truths to every situation in our lives.

If, at this juncture, there exists the slight possibility you have not been challenged to evaluate or reevaluate the impact that Scripture is called to play in your life as a follower of Christ, here are a few points I will ask you to consider.

I'll start by asking, "Is there such a thing as an atheist?" This is a trick question, but I'll humor you with my answer by emphasizing the importance and authority of Scripture. While we know millions of people identify as atheists, according to Scripture, there is no such person. Romans 1:19 states, *"They (mankind) know the truth about God because he has made it obvious to them."* (NLT). The literal interpretation suggests that there is an innate part of man that knows there's a God (general revelation), and therefore, no such person as an atheist. Those who identify as atheists, therefore, must be made aware that continued denial of what they know to be innately true could result in what Scripture calls being turned over by the Lord to a reprobate mind (Romans 1:28). This is where the self-labeled atheist can't connect to the God they know exists in their heart. Famous atheist and author of "The Age of Reason," Thomas Paine's last words on his death bed confirm this point. A witness said Thomas Paine desperately uttered, *"I would give worlds if I had them, that the Age of Reason had never been published. O, Lord, help me! Christ, help me! No, don't leave; stay with me! Send even a child to stay with me, for I am on the edge of Hell here alone. If ever the Devil had an agent, I have been that one."*

My point is that, as believers, we let Scripture take authority over man's finite labels, opinions, and faulty beliefs. Scripture's truth helps believers confront unbelief through the innate part of all men who know God. This is where we trust special revelation in Jesus, revealing Himself to the part of us that knows God exists. Ephesians 2:8-9 reads, *"For by grace you have been saved through faith, and that not of yourselves; it is the gift of God, not of works, lest anyone should boast."* (NKJV). At this moment we should all shout "Hallelujah!" "And glory to His name" because the Lord has revealed Himself to us. We didn't choose Him; He chose us, and to that end, we can't take credit for our salvation. The point here is simple: the literal truth of Scripture brings clarity to life. Our Psalmist understands this truth, so much so that the Word of God is paramount in his soul.

When we approach God's Word with the same understanding as our Psalmist, we can faithfully apply its literal truth to our daily lives. As you continue this reading, ask God to show you where His Word needs to permeate your heart and mind so that it is evident in your daily thoughts and actions. Pray that the Lord will provide clarity if any place in your life is disconnected from His truth. Pray that you will follow the Lord's instructions to Joshua, *"...be strong and very courageous, that you may observe to do according to all the law which Moses My servant commanded you; do not turn from it to the right hand or to the left, that you may prosper wherever you go. This Book of the Law shall not depart from your mouth, but you shall meditate in it day and night, that you may observe to do according to all that is written in it. For then you will make your way prosperous, and then you will have good success."* (Joshua 1:8-9 NKJV).

When we challenge ourselves to follow God's Word of truth and make its application paramount in our lives, we become the disciples indeed (John 8:31) that Jesus calls us to be. It is then that the Scriptures declare we experience the *"good success"* that God promises Joshua. Jesus says in John 7:38, *"He who believes in Me, as the Scripture has said, out of his heart will flow rivers of living water."* (NKJV). The only way to become the disciples indeed who flow rivers of living water is to follow God's **precepts, testimony, commandments, judgments, ways, laws, statutes,** and **Word** with Christ as our way, truth, and life. (John 14:6).

As you approach these next eleven days, it is my hope and prayer that the Psalmist will challenge you to the Significance, Relevance, Richness, and Authority of God's Word. I pray that if the Psalmist has not impacted or challenged your approach to God's Word in a profound way, there will be a paradigm shift in your mind, heart, and spirit to walk down **"The Road Less Traveled."**

"Joyful are those who obey God's laws and search for him with all their hearts" (Psalm 119:2).

MY PRAYER

Lord, please continue to bless those who are endeavoring to take this challenge. Lord, I pray that we all are not just hearers of Your Word but that we become true doers of Your Word. That Your Word travels from our minds to our hearts and takes root there, manifesting in our daily actions.

Lord, I pray that we all are being transformed by the renewing of our minds and that we bring glory and honor to Your name and the Kingdom of Jesus Christ. Please, Lord, birth in all a desire to cry aloud, "Oh, that my actions would consistently reflect your decrees! (119:5).

Lord, I pray this prayer in the mighty and matchless name of Jesus Christ. Amen!

THE 22-DAY CHALLENGE
PART TWO

DAY #12: LAMEDH

89. Your eternal word, O Lord, stands firm in heaven.

90. Your faithfulness extends to every generation, as enduring as the earth you created.

91. Your regulations remain true to this day, for everything serves your plans.

92. If your instructions hadn't sustained me with joy, I would have died in my misery.

93. I will never forget your commandments, for by them you give me life.

94. I am yours; rescue me! For I have worked hard at obeying your commandments.

95. Though the wicked hide along the way to kill me, I will quietly keep my mind on your laws.

96. Even perfection has its limits, but your commands have no limit.

QUESTIONS

1. Read verse 90 and consider what you have done to extend God's Word to the next generation. What more will you do?

2. In verse 91, the psalmist says that everything serves God's plans. Today think about world situations on a macro and micro level and consider how everything serves the Lord's plans. Read Proverbs 16:33, Romans 8:28, Ephesians 1:11, Colossians 1:16-17.

3. Today think of all the troubles of the world and then think of your troubles and concerns, then read verses 92 & 93. Amid your troubles and concerns does God's Word bring you joy, now consider what sustains your life? Give the Lord thanks today that His Word brings joy and sustains us even amid the troubles of this life! Read John 10:10.

4. Take a moment of meditation and consider that the Lord's commands have no limit in our lives (verse 96).

JOURNAL

Notes- Thoughts- Meditations- Insights

DAY #13: MEM

97. Oh, how I love your instructions! I think about them all day long.

98. Your commands make me wiser than my enemies, for they are my constant guide.

99. Yes, I have more insight than my teachers, for I am always thinking of your laws.

100. I am even wiser than my elders, for I have kept your commandments.

101. I have refused to walk on any evil path, so that I may remain obedient to your word.

102. I haven't turned away from your regulations, for you have taught me well.

103. How sweet your words taste to me; they are sweeter than honey.

104. Your commandments give me understanding; no wonder I hate every false way of life.

QUESTIONS

1. **In verse 97, the psalmist exclaims that he loves the Lord's instructions. Do you share this same love of God's Word? Think of the reasons why you love God's Word. Make a list of 3-5 reasons why you love God's Word. Read Psalm 1.**

2. Read verses 99-100, can you think of a time when you were wiser than your teachers and elders? What made you wiser? Was it that you followed the Lord's instructions? Think of the reasons for your wisdom and the situations where you followed God's Word above worldly wisdom.

3. In lieu of the first two questions, meditate on the meaning of verse 103. What thoughts resonate in your spirit?

4. In verse 104, the psalmist mentions a false way of life. As you look at the world today, can you identify false ways of life? Now, consider how God's Word helps us avoid these false ways.

JOURNAL

Notes- Thoughts- Meditations- Insights

PSALM 119
THE ROAD LESS TRAVELED

DAY #14: NUN

105. Your word is a lamp to guide my feet and a light for my path.

106. I've promised it once, and I'll promise it again: I will obey your righteous regulations.

107. I have suffered much, O Lord; restore my life again as you promised.

108. Lord, accept my offering of praise, and teach me your regulations.

109. My life constantly hangs in the balance, but I will not stop obeying your instructions.

110. The wicked have set their traps for me, but I will not turn from your commandments.

111. Your laws are my treasure; they are my heart's delight.

112. I am determined to keep your decrees to the very end.

QUESTIONS

1. **Verse 105 says that God's Word is to lead and guide us as believers. Do you share this interpretation? In what ways does God's Word lead you in navigating the social, political, and cultural constructs of our heavily immoral and divided society and culture?**

2. In verse 106 the psalmist promises to obey the Lord's righteous regulations. When faced with believers who have compromised the Lord's righteous regulations and have bowed to cultural constructs such as racism, legalism, and nationalism, how have you promised to obey God's Word? In what ways do you need to repent or be strengthened in your resolve to press on to be obedient to the righteous regulations of the Lord? Read Phil. 4:12-14.

3. Reflect on the first two questions and meditate on the meaning of verse 109. What thoughts resonate in your spirit?

4. Be introspective and honest with yourself and God today and think of the times and ways you have fallen short of obeying God's Word. Now think of ways that you can say with confidence, *"Your word is a lamp to guide my feet and a light for my path"* (verse 105), *"I will obey your righteous regulations"* (verse 106), *"I will not stop obeying your instructions"* (verse 109), *"I will not turn from your commandments"* (verse 110), *"I am determined to keep your decrees to the very end"* (verse 112).

JOURNAL

Notes- Thoughts- Meditations- Insights

PSALM 119
THE ROAD LESS TRAVELED

DAY #15: SAMEKH

113. I hate those with divided loyalties, but I love your instructions.

114. You are my refuge and my shield; your word is my source of hope.

115. Get out of my life, you evil-minded people, for I intend to obey the commands of my God.

116. Lord, sustain me as you promised, that I may live! Do not let my hope be crushed.

117. Sustain me, and I will be rescued; then I will meditate continually on your decrees.

118. But you have rejected all who stray from your decrees. They are only fooling themselves.

119. You skim off the wicked of the earth like scum; no wonder I love to obey your laws!

120. I tremble in fear of you; I stand in awe of your regulations.

QUESTIONS

1. **In verse 113, the psalmist refers to those with divided loyalties; in verse 115, he tells evil-minded people to get out of his life. Do you have anyone close to you with divided loyalties to the point where you may have to distance yourself for your own spiritual welfare? Today think about those**

around you and how they affect your spiritual life and walk with the Lord.

2. When it comes to those in your life who profess Christ but do not live Christ, how might you give them the psalmist's advice in verse 118? How might you tell them they are only fooling themselves?

3. Two times in this section, the psalmist asks the Lord to "sustain him" (vv. 116 &117). Meditate on how God and His Word have sustained you and give Him thanks for specific times of His sustaining love.

4. Consider the last verse in this section (120) and ask yourself if you share the psalmist's reverent fear. Is that fear enough to "stand in awe of Your (the Lord's) regulations?" Read Psalm 8:3-4, Psalm 33:8-9, Psalm 100:1-5.

JOURNAL

Notes- Thoughts- Meditations- Insights

PSALM 119
THE ROAD LESS TRAVELED

DAY #16: AYIN

121. Don't leave me to the mercy of my enemies, for I have done what is just and right.

122. Please guarantee a blessing for me. Don't let the arrogant oppress me!

123. My eyes strain to see your rescue, to see the truth of your promise fulfilled.

124. I am your servant; deal with me in unfailing love, and teach me your decrees.

125. Give discernment to me, your servant; then I will understand your laws.

126. Lord, it is time for you to act, for these evil people have violated your instructions.

127. Truly, I love your commands more than gold, even the finest gold.

128. Each of your commandments is right. That is why I hate every false way.

QUESTIONS

1. **In verse 122, the psalmist mentions arrogant people who oppress. How do you deal with these kinds of people? Is it biblical or carnal? Read Colossians 3:13, Ephesians 4:2.**

2. In verse 125, the psalmist asks the Lord for discernment: is this something that you pray for? Consider how important discernment is in dealing with difficult people and situations. Consider how godly discernment could help as it pertains to question #1.

3. Reflect on verse 126 and the subject of dealing with difficult people. Do you yield to the Lord to deal with them in His timing, or do you take matters into your own hands? Consider the appropriate biblical response to dealing with evil people who violate God's instructions. Read Proverbs 15:1, Matthew 5:44, James 3:13-16.

4. In verse 127, the psalmist alludes to the commands of the Lord being as valuable as the finest gold. Do you share that assumption? In what ways have you placed the commands of the Lord as valuable and precious in your life?

JOURNAL

Notes- Thoughts- Meditations- Insights

PSALM 119
THE ROAD LESS TRAVELED

DAY #17: PE

129. Your laws are wonderful. No wonder I obey them!

130. The teaching of your word gives light, so even the simple can understand.

131. I pant with expectation, longing for your commands.

132. Come and show me your mercy, as you do for all who love your name.

133. Guide my steps by your word, so I will not be overcome by evil.

134. Ransom me from the oppression of evil people; then I can obey your commandments.

135. Look upon me with love; teach me your decrees.

136. Rivers of tears gush from my eyes because people disobey your instructions.

QUESTIONS

1. **Contrast and compare verses 133 & 136. Lament, meditate, and pray for those who disobey the Lord's instructions.**

2. **Pray for one person who you know professes Christ but does not obey His instructions. Consider ways that you might help him/her follow Christ in spirit and truth.**

3. Today, consider praying for someone who knows nothing about God's Word. Pray for those you would consider evil (v. 134) and how you may influence them with and through God's Word.

4. Ask the Lord to guide your steps (v. 133) so that you will not be overcome with evil and that He will lead you to someone who needs to hear about the goodness of God and His Word. Read Matthew 28:19-20 & 2 Timothy 3:16-17.

JOURNAL

Notes- Thoughts- Meditations- Insights

PSALM 119
THE ROAD LESS TRAVELED

DAY 18: TSADHE

137. Lord, you are righteous, and your regulations are fair.

138. Your laws are perfect and completely trustworthy.

139. I am overwhelmed with indignation, for my enemies have disregarded your words.

140. Your promises have been thoroughly tested; that is why I love them so much.

141. I am insignificant and despised, but I don't forget your commandments.

142. Your justice is eternal, and your instructions are perfectly true.

143. As pressure and stress bear down on me, I find joy in your commands.

144. Your laws are always right; help me to understand them so I may live.

QUESTIONS

1. **In verse 138, the psalmist declares God's laws as perfect; however, in a world that legalizes immorality, do you share in this belief? If not, how do you rectify your beliefs with the Word of God? Examples: same-sex marriage, abortion.**

2. Combine question #1 and verse 139 and consider the divisive climate of our times. Now consider how you react to people, churches or organizations that disregard God's Word. Is your response biblical, and if not, how has this challenge changed your view?

3. When the pressure and stress of family, church, and culture bear down on you, do you find joy in God's Word? What specific Scriptures and or books bring you joy and why? Today, send a struggling friend or co-worker a verse or group of passages that have brought you joy.

4. Today, consider the challenge; if it has helped you appreciate God's Word even more, pay the challenge forward and give a copy to a friend!

JOURNAL

Notes- Thoughts- Meditations- Insights

PSALM 119
THE ROAD LESS TRAVELED

DAY #19: QOPH

145. I pray with all my heart; answer me, Lord! I will obey your decrees.

146. I cry out to you; rescue me, that I may obey your laws.

147. I rise early, before the sun is up; I cry out for help and put my hope in your words.

148. I stay awake through the night, thinking about your promise.

149. In your faithful love, O Lord, hear my cry; let me be revived by following your regulations.

150. Lawless people are coming to attack me; they live far from your instructions.

151. But you are near, O Lord, and all your commands are true.

152. I have known from my earliest days that your laws will last forever.

QUESTIONS

1. **In verses 145-150, the psalmist seems to be struggling here amid tribulation. Do you meditate on God's Word in times of trouble? Do you completely trust God's Word during the times when evil people seem to have the upper hand? Read Psalm 23, Proverbs 3:5-6.**

2. Can you, like the psalmist, come to the same conclusion in verse 151? Read Psalm 118:6, Matthew 28:20, Hebrews 4:16, Hebrews 13:5-6.

3. Consider the times when you knew it was the Lord Who heard your cry. Now read verse 148 and meditate on your thoughts about the promises of God.

4. In verse 152, the psalmist reminds us that God's Word (laws) will last forever. Now consider the hope and joy that the Word brings to your life! Read Hebrews 13:8.

JOURNAL

Notes- Thoughts- Meditations- Insights

DAY #20: RESH

153. Look upon my suffering and rescue me, for I have not forgotten your instructions.

154. Argue my case; take my side! Protect my life as you promised.

155. The wicked are far from rescue, for they do not bother with your decrees.

156. Lord, how great is your mercy; let me be revived by following your regulations.

157. Many persecute and trouble me, yet I have not swerved from your laws.

158. Seeing these traitors makes me sick at heart, because they care nothing for your word.

159. See how I love your commandments, Lord. Give back my life because of your unfailing love.

160. The very essence of your words is truth; all your just regulations will stand forever.

QUESTIONS

1. **In verses 153 and 154, the psalmist pleads for rescue and protection. Think back to a time when the Lord did that for you. Now think of how that is consistent with the Scriptures. What passages come to mind regarding the Lord's promise of protection and rescue? Read Psalm 91:1-2.**

2. In verse 155, the psalmist points to the antithesis of protection for the wicked. Can you think back to a time before your salvation when you did not enjoy the Lord's protection and rescue? Take a moment to thank the Lord for rescuing you from sin and death! Read Romans 10:9-10, John 3:16- 18.

3. Reflect on verse 159. Now consider how the Lord brought you back to life through His Son, Jesus Christ, and your salvation. Read Ephesians 2:8-9, John 3:16, John 10:10.

4. Meditate on verse 160 and consider the world's ever-changing moral and societal views. Now, think about how God's unchanging Word could benefit those who adore the sin of the world. Who can you touch today with the unchanging truth contained in God's forever Word?

JOURNAL

Notes- Thoughts- Meditations- Insights

PSALM 119
THE ROAD LESS TRAVELED

DAY #21: SHIN

161. Powerful people harass me without cause, but my heart trembles only at your word.

162. I rejoice in your word like one who discovers a great treasure.

163. I hate and abhor all falsehood, but I love your instructions.

164. I will praise you seven times a day because all your regulations are just.

165. Those who love your instructions have great peace and do not stumble.

166. I long for your rescue, Lord, so I have obeyed your commands.

167. I have obeyed your laws, for I love them very much.

168. Yes, I obey your commandments and laws because you know everything I do.

QUESTIONS

1. **In verse 161, the psalmist's confidence is solely in God's Word. Do you share this same confidence so much that you are not worried about the schemes of powerful people?**

2. Read verse 164 and consider how many times a day you praise the Lord for His regulations. Will you commit to giving Him even more praise for His holy and righteous Word?

3. Do you have great peace because you treasure the Word of the Lord? Read and reflect on verse 165.

4. Meditate on verse 168 and consider how many in Christ live as if the Lord does not see all they do. Consider how some sins may be accepted by man but will be judged by the Lord. Considering that the Lord sees all we do, is your life ready for the judgment seat?

JOURNAL

Notes- Thoughts- Meditations- Insights

DAY #22: TAW

169. Lord, listen to my cry; give me the discerning mind you promised.

170. Listen to my prayer; rescue me as you promised.

171. Let praise flow from my lips, for you have taught me your decrees.

172. Let my tongue sing about your word, for all your commands are right.

173. Give me a helping hand, for I have chosen to follow your commandments.

174. O Lord, I have longed for your rescue, and your instructions are my delight.

175. Let me live so I can praise you, and may your regulations help me.

176. I have wandered away like a lost sheep; come and find me, for I have not forgotten your commands.

QUESTIONS

1. **Read verses 171 & 172 and consider how you praise God for His Word. What practical ways do you give thanks to God for this Word that brings life? Read John 6:63, Hebrews 4:12.**

2. In verse 173, the psalmist says that God's commandments are like a helping hand. How would you agree? Why?

3. Read verse 175 and consider how your life praises the Lord because His regulations help you daily.

4. Now that you have reached the end of this lengthy Psalm, reflect deeply on how you will never forget (verse 176) this experience with sole emphasis on the *commands, precepts, laws, regulations, testimonies, judgments, ways, statutes,* and Word of Almighty God.

JOURNAL

Notes- Thoughts- Meditations- Insights

AUTHOR'S INSIGHT

The following is a newsletter article I wrote for Tiger Pause Youth Ministry, where I serve as Director of Ministry. I hope it will provide insight into how I apply God's Word in my ministry and daily living. John 8:31-32, *"Then said Jesus to those Jews which believed on him, if ye continue in my word, then are ye my disciples; indeed, and ye shall know the truth, and the truth shall make you free."* (KJV).

"DON'T LOSE YOUR FOCUS"

Last week, I preached a sermon from Matthew 14, verses 22-33, entitled *"Don't lose your focus."* If these passages don't immediately come to mind, let me refresh your memory and tell you that this is right after Jesus feeds the multitude and immediately after He tells the disciples to get into a boat and meet Him on the other side of the sea (lake). The passages go on to say that the disciples meet rough seas and are struggling and afraid. This is when Jesus shows up and tells the disciples, *"Be of good cheer! It is I; do not be afraid."* (Matthew 14:27). Unafraid, Peter then asks Jesus if he could come to Him walking on the water. When Jesus tells Peter to come, most of us are familiar with this part of the story. Peter begins to walk on the water and is fine as long as he keeps his focus on Jesus. The second Peter took his eyes off Christ, most of us know, he almost drowned.

I want us to focus on these passages as we examine the current state of Christianity at large, especially here in America. I say this because I believe that, in some regards, we have taken our focus off Jesus. Now, I understand that this may not be a shared opinion of all, but as we continue to see churches closing, pastors quitting, and membership declining, we must pinpoint the reasons these realities exist. I submit that one reason for our current state is that we have let the world define many of the moral issues that confront our culture, and the church has become a thermometer of the world, recording the current ideologies and opinions of the present society. As Martin Luther King once said, for the body of Christ to be holy (set apart to do God's will), we must be thermostats, regulators, that influence culture and society.

Let us take one issue confronting our culture and filter it through the prism (reflector of light) of God's Word. I think most Christians would agree that abortion is morally wrong according to the Word of God. Let's just start with *"Thou shall not kill"* (Exodus 20:13) and the fact that God knew us before we were in our mothers' wombs (Jeremiah 1:5). With our focus on Scripture, abortion is a moral issue before it is a legal issue. I say this because many in the body of Christ view the legality of abortion as a central issue when it comes to their political decisions. However, I would point out that as we focus on Scripture, it tells us to *"Go ye therefore and teach all nations."* (Matthew 28:19). Excuse my feeble attempt at sarcasm, but how about we teach people this silly notion, "That you're not supposed to have sex before marriage?" If we would focus on Christ and His Word, we would understand that it is better to TEACH morality than to legislate it. Now, I'm not saying that we shouldn't vote our Bibles; however, what I am saying is that, as the church, we must stop focusing on CNN and

PSALM 119
THE ROAD LESS TRAVELED

Fox News or the culture as our means for interpreting our views on issues that confront the church and culture. Romans 12:2 tells us that we are not to be world conformed but Word TRANSFORMED by the renewing of our minds. When we focus on Scripture and reject conformity to the world's twisted morality, we become the thermostats that God's Word and Martin Luther King calls for us to be. I will close with three points to ponder with our earlier stated Matthew 14 passages in mind.

1. **DON'T BE AFRAID:**

As believers of Jesus, we cannot be afraid to go against the grain when other Christians get off the mark. We must let our biblically flavored voices be heard. A lot can be said about Peter almost drowning. But let it also be said that he was the only disciple who had courage enough to step out on faith and get out of the boat. While our opinions may not be popular, it is Jesus Himself who says to us, *"Be of good cheer! It is I; do not be afraid."* Silence in twisted morality equals complicity, and the world's popular opinion is how we end up with things like abortion, slavery, and racism.

2. **STEP OUT ON FAITH:**

As I just pointed out, Peter was the only disciple courageous enough to step out of the boat during the storm. His testing was a storm of perfection, and Jesus was preparing Peter to trust in Him. The perfecting of Peter's faith is evident as we know he went on to do remarkable things for the Lord. His storm of perfection is quite different from Jonah's storm of correction for being disobedient to the Lord. We know Jonah's disobedience led to his ending up in the belly of a great fish. The body of Christ and we, as individual believers, must decide if this moment in redemption history is a storm of perfection or a storm of correction. I believe that, because it is Jesus Who is with us, we can and we must step out on faith and define the issues that confront us with the Word of God, even if it's not popular.

3. DON'T LOSE YOUR FOCUS:

We must know the power of the One Who says, *"He will never leave us nor forsake us."* (Hebrews 13:5). If God is for us, then who can be against us? (Romans 8:31). Yes, I will agree that we live in a complicated world and in a complicated time. However, I submit that it only becomes complicated when we take our focus off Jesus Christ. Jesus' teachings were revolutionary. So much so that we know that the Jewish culture rejected Him by crucifixion. We must know Who is with us. We can't be like the disciples in the storm of Matthew 8. That's when Jesus is with them in the boat, and when the roughness of the sea caused them to be frightened, they go to Jesus and cry, *"Master, we perish."* (Matthew 8:24). When Jesus calmed the seas, they conclude, *"What manner of a man is this that even the winds and seas obey Him"* Matthew 8:27). This statement tells us that they didn't know Who Jesus was. However, in the storm of our Matthew 14 text, after the seas are calm, the disciples worship Jesus because they know now Who He is: the Son of the living God. Let us also focus on Who He is and worship Him in spirit and truth.

CONCLUSION

We, as the body of Christ, faced with all the complexities of the 21st century, must not lose our focus. The issues that confront our culture and society are not as complicated as the world may make them out to be. If the body of Christ were compelled to be transformed by the Word instead of conformed to the culture, maybe we would see a revival across our country and the world. The continued deteriorating state of Christianity in our culture must be a primary concern of the church, and while you may agree or disagree with my examination, we cannot ignore our current state. To not acknowledge our decline is losing focus of reality and not reaching for the available hand of Jesus, Who is there to save us.

Humbly submitted by,
Rev. Dr. Bryan Crawl

FINAL THOUGHTS

Now that you have completed the 22-day challenge, the real lifelong test begins or continues. The daily engagement of God's Word is with, as I like to say, "an eye to apply." This journey will begin and continue if you have indeed been challenged through this time of biblical study, meditation, and reflection.

Someone once told me that the longest nine inches known to man are the nine inches between the mind and the heart. Therefore, there can exist a gulf between our orthodoxy (knowledge of sound doctrine) and our orthopraxy (sound application). The real challenge becomes to live our daily lives bridging the gulf. In John 8:31-32, believers have received these instructions from our Lord, *"Then said Jesus to those Jews which believed on him, "If ye continue in my word, then are ye my disciples; indeed, and ye shall know the truth, and the truth shall make you free." (KJV)*.

There's something I like to say to my congregants that I will now share with you, *"Everybody wants to be a Christian, but nobody wants to be a Christian."* What I mean by that is many want Jesus as Savior, but not all will follow Him as Lord. When we talk about "The Road Less Traveled" it is less traveled because many will follow what they think is the right way; however, we are reminded that it is only Jesus Christ Who is the way, the truth, and the life, and that our thinking is finite. Therefore, to truly follow Jesus is to live out the Words contained in 119:105, *"Your word is a lamp to guide my feet and a light for my path." (NLT)*. I believe this means that we must get out of our own way, out of our own thinking, and out of our own flawed beliefs and let the Word of God lead and guide us. When we follow Jesus, He will lead us to be His disciples indeed.

Thank you for indulging in my efforts to heighten our spiritual senses to the leading of the Scriptures in our lives. My prayer is that, above all, we shed the shackles of worldly thinking and constructs and truly give God's Word the place it deserves in our daily lives. My prayer is that this offering produces a hunger that knows, *"How sweet are your words to my taste, sweeter than honey to my mouth!"* Psalm 119:103 NLT. My desire for all God's people is that traversing the Word of God will never be "The Road Less Traveled."

MY PRAYER

Lord, I pray that this reader's worldview and Word view have been heightened as they complete this portion of Your Word. Lord, I pray that this reader will continue in Your Word and be Your disciple indeed and that the truth of Scripture will set them free of anything that would keep them from fulfilling Your precepts, testimony, commandments, judgments, ways, laws, and statutes.

Lord, I pray that this reader would challenge others in Word and deed to endeavor also to take this challenge and that the entire body of Christ might be resolved to take up our crosses daily and follow our soon-coming King in spirit and in truth.

Lord, I pray that Your Word would be a lamp to our feet and an ever-present light in our path (119:105) and that we would have the heart to cry out, "I have refused to walk on any evil path, so that I may remain obedient to your word." (119:101). Lord, I pray that we all would be dutiful to Your Word and diligently pursue "The Road Less Traveled!"

I pray this prayer in the mighty and matchless name of Jesus Christ. Amen!

ABOUT THE AUTHOR

    Rev. Dr. Bryan Crawl is a retired Air Force firefighter who proudly served our country for 26 years. He currently resides in Rochester, Pa., where he is the Senior Pastor of the Second Baptist Church. He is also the Director of the Ministry for Tiger Pause Youth Ministry located in neighboring Beaver Falls, Pa. As an active member of his community, Rev. Crawl is an assistant coach for the Beaver Falls High School golf team and is a member of Beaver County "Undivided," an organization whose goal is racial reconciliation of churches and communities.

    Rev. Crawl attended Geneva College of Beaver Falls, Pa., earning a Bachelor of Science degree in Community Ministry. He also attended Grand Canyon University, earning a Master of Arts degree in Christian Studies with an emphasis on pastoral ministry. In 2020, Rev. Crawl earned his Doctor of Ministry degree from Covington Theological Seminary in Ft. Oglethorpe, GA. Rev. Crawl is married to the love of his life, Apryl, and is the loving father of Crystal, Bianca, and Christian and the proud grandfather of Dre V. and Cali G. On his tombstone, Rev. Crawl would like to have cemented "RWG Bryan K. Crawl lover of God and the people of God!"

REFERENCES

Evans, T. (2020). The Tony Evans study Bible (First ed. Holman Bible Publishers.

King, M. L., Rev. Dr. (1977). Strength to love (2010th ed. Collins + World; Fortress Press.

Lewis, C. (1958). Reflection on the Psalms (First ed). Harper Collins.

*NOTE: The Scriptures used for the challenge were from the New Living Translation. All other translations used were identified.

Made in the USA
Las Vegas, NV
19 February 2025